The Return Ritual

By A.E. Mickey

Vuelve A Ti™ Ritual House

Published by **Vuelve A Ti Press**

Vuelve A Ti™ Ritual House is an imprint of
Vuelve A Ti Press

ISBN: 979-8-9996781-2-6

This guide is for inspirational and educational purposes only. It is not intended as medical, psychological, or mental health advise, diagnosis, or treatment. If you are experiencing a mental health crisis, seek professional support or contact local emergency services.

First Edition, 2026
Printed in the United States of America

A Gentle Note

This guide is for inspirational and educational purposes only and is not medical, psychological, or mental health treatment.

If you are experiencing a mental health crisis, please seek professional support or contact local emergency services.

Hello Beautiful Soul,

You've been holding everyone together. You've been the strong one. The responsible one. The one who handles it.
And somewhere along the way, you stopped feeling like you. I see you.

This is not a self improvement program.
This is not a glow up challenge.
This is not another thing you need to "do perfectly."

This is a return.

Seven days. Ten minutes a day.
Soft ritual. Sacred devotion.
A place to set the weight down.

You don't have to fix your whole life this week.
You only have to remember yourself.

Welcome home,
Eli
Founder, Vuelve A Ti
Author of The Web You Weave

How to Use This Ritual

Each day is 10 minutes.

What you'll do:

1. Prepare (1 minute)
2. Breath + Touch (2 minutes)
3. Ritual Step (3 minutes)
4. Journal Prompt (3 minutes)
5. Seal (1 minute)

What you'll need:

- a cup of warm tea or water
- a candle (optional)
- a pen and a journal (you can use your notes app)
- one skincare product, oil OR lotion (anything you already have)

You do not need expensive products. This is about intention.

The Sacred Rule

Do not rush.

Even if you only do 4 minutes, you completed the ritual.

The point is not performance.
The point is return.

What You May Notice

During this ritual, you may notice:

- emotions surfacing unexpectedly
- fatigue the first few days
- a sense of quiet or spaciousness
- tears without a clear reason
- a desire to move slower

This is normal. Your system is coming out of survival mode. You are not doing it wrong.

You are returning.

Day 1 RETURN.

You may feel more grounded or aware of how tired you've been.

Theme: "I am here. I am back."

What you're reclaiming: Presence

Prepare (1 minute)
Place one hand on your chest, the other hand on your belly.

Say: "I am here."

Breath + Touch (2 minutes)

Inhale through the nose for a count of 4.
Hold for a count of 2.
Exhale for a count of 6.

Gently rub your palms together to create warmth.
Then place your warm palms over your face like a blessing.

Repeat once more as you tilt your face towards the sky.
Say: **"I am here, I am peace."**

Ritual (3 minutes)

Apply your moisturizer / oil slowly.

As your hands move, say:
"I return to myself."
"I belong to me again."
"My body is safe with me."

Journal (3 minutes)

Write without thinking:

- Where have I been living lately. My mind, my fear, my stress, my duty?

- What does my body need from me right now?

Seal (1 minute)

Whisper: **"I have returned."**

Day 2 REPAIR

You may feel softer, emotional, or more sensitive.

Theme: "I soften. I mend."

What you're reclaiming: Safety

Prepare

Pour yourself a warm drink. It could be a cup of tea, or warm water with lemon. Hold it with two hands and take a sip.

Breath + Touch (2 minutes)

Inhale for a count of 4, exhale for a count of 8. Long exhale tells the nervous system; ***you're safe.***

Ritual (3 minutes)

Gently massage your neck, your jaw and shoulders.

Then apply your product and say:

"I am allowed to heal."
"It is safe to soften."
"I do not have to be hard to survive."

Journal

- What part of me has been hardened by life?

- What would softness look like in one small way this week?

Seal

Whisper **"I repair what life has disrupted."**

Day 3
WORTH

You may notice self talk shifting.

Theme: “I do not earn love.”

What you’re reclaiming: Value

Prepare:
Stand in front of a mirror

Breath + Touch

Inhale for a count of 4, hold for 2, exhale for 6.
Look at yourself without fixing anything.

Ritual

As you apply your skincare, look into your own eyes.

Say:

“I am on time.”
“I am enough.”
“I am easy to love.”
“I am worthy.”

Journal

- Where did I learn I had to earn love?

- What is one thing I admire about the woman in the mirror?

Seal

"I remember my worth."

Day 4
RELEASE

You may feel lighter, clearer, or aware of what you're ready to let go of.

Theme: "I set the weight down."

What you're reclaiming: Freedom

Prepare
Write down 3 burdens on a scrap paper (you can use your notes app)

Breath + Touch
Inhale for a count of 4. Exhale for a count of 8.
On each exhale imagine weight leaving your shoulders.

Ritual
Apply product with feather light strokes.

Say:

"I release what is not mine."
"I release the pressure."
"I release the role of carrying everything."

Journal

- What burden am I carrying that isn't mine?"
- What would change if I stopped carrying it?"

Seal

Rip or delete the list and say

"I release it. I am free."

Day 5
RADIANCE

You may notice a quiet confidence or a desire to show up more fully.

Theme: "I allow myself to be seen."

What you're reclaiming: Glow + Visibility

Prepare

Put on one thing that makes you feel feminine (lip balm counts)

Breath + Touch

Inhale through your nose
Exhale through your mouth like a sigh.

Ritual

Massage your cheeks upward as you apply your skincare.

Say:

"My radiance is not arrogance."
"My light's brightness is a beacon."
"I was made to shine."

Journal

- Where have I dimmed myself?"
- What part of my power am I ready to reclaim?

Seal

Extend your arms out to either side of your body, look up and say
"I allow my light to shine fully."

Day 6
PROTECTION

You may feel more discerning about your energy, time and access to you.

Theme: "Not everything gets access to me."

What you're reclaiming: Boundaries

Prepare

Place a small object near you (it could be a ring, a necklace, a stone) This object is your boundary symbol

Breath + Touch

Inhale for a count of 4. Hold for a count of 2. Exhale for a count of 6.

Ritual

Apply your skin care product and imagine a veil around you.

Say:

“I am protected.”
“I am guided.”
“I choose what gets access to me.”
“I am allowed to say no.”

Journal

- What drains me the most?
- What boundary would protect my peace?

Seal

Touch your symbol object and say.

“I protect my peace.”

Day 7
DEVOTION

You may experience a deep sense of self trust or reconnection with your inner steadiness.

Theme: " I am mine"

What you're reclaiming: Commitment to self.

Prepare

Light a candle (optional). Sit on the floor or a chair. Place your hands gently on your thighs, palms facing up. Sit still.

Breath + Touch

Inhale for a count of 4. Exhale for a count of 8. Repeat this for two minutes. With your last inhale gently bring your hands up and place them on your heart, in the middle of your chest keeping your palms open then exhale.

Ritual

Still in your sitting position take your skin care and apply it slowly.

Say:
"I choose myself."
"I will not abandon me."
"I am the love of my own life."
"I return again and again."

Journal

- What does devotion to myself look like?

- What promise am I making to me?

Seal

Write and sign this;

I, _________________________, return to myself.

Signature: __________ Date: ____________

You did it.

Look at you. I'm so proud of the woman who just showed up for herself.

Not because your life magically changed in seven days, but because you returned.

And when a woman returns to herself, she moves differently. She chooses differently. She carries herself differently.

Welcome home.

Eli

Notes

Notes

You can return to this ritual
whenever you need yourself again.

About the Author

A.E. Mickey (know to many as Eli) is the author of *The Web You Weave* and the founder of Vuelve A Ti - a body of work devoted to emotional return, nervous system safety, and guiding women back to themselves through ritual, reflection, and lived wisdom.

Her work supports women who have carried too much for too long; offering grounded pathways back to safety, self trust, and inner steadiness.

Made in the USA
Las Vegas, NV
01 February 2026

40920261R00016